Multicultural Crafts
Kids Can Do!

American Indian Crafts Kids Can Do!

Carol Gnojewski

Enslow Elementary
an imprint of
Enslow Publishers, Inc.

40 Industrial Road   PO Box 38
Box 398   Aldershot
Berkeley Heights, NJ 07922   Hants GU12 6BP
USA   UK

http://www.enslow.com

Enslow Elementary, an imprint of Enslow Publishers, Inc.

Enslow Elementary® is a registered trademark of Enslow Publishers, Inc.

Library of Congress Cataloging-in-Publication Data

Gnojewski, Carol.
   American Indian crafts kids can do! / Carol Gnojewski.
      p. cm. — (Multicultural crafts kids can do!)
   Includes bibliographical references and index.
   ISBN 0-7660-2458-X
   1. Indian craft—Juvenile literature. 2. Indians of North America—
Industries—United States—Juvenile literature. I. Title. II. Series.
TT23.G52 2006
745.5089'97—dc22

                                    2005028116

Printed in the United States of America

10 9 8 7 6 5 4 3 2 1

To Our Readers: We have done our best to make sure all Internet Addresses in this
book were active and appropriate when we went to press. However, the author and the
publisher have no control over and assume no liability for the material available on those
Internet sites or on other Web sites they may link to. Any comments or suggestions can
be sent by e-mail to comments@enslow.com or to the address on the back cover.

Every effort has been made to locate all copyright holders of material
used in this book. If any errors or omissions have occurred,
corrections will be made in future editions of this book.

Illustration Credits: Crafts prepared by June
Ponte; photography by Lindsay Pries. Corel
Corporation, pp. 4, 5, 10, 16.

Cover Illustration: Photography by
Lindsay Pries.

Contents

Safety Note: Be sure to ask for help from
an adult, if needed, to
complete these crafts!

Introduction

American Indians of all ages, from tribes across North America, took time for play just as we do now. Each tribe may have had unique toys and games, though games were often shared as tribes met to trade and to learn from each other. Some of their toys are still familiar to us, such as dolls, balls, and toy animals. They were crafted from local materials, but could be as simple or as fancy as toys are today.

Many toys taught survival skills, such as toy boats, toy homes, and toy weapons. Many were crafted just as the

These boots and moccasins were made by Indians from the Arctic.

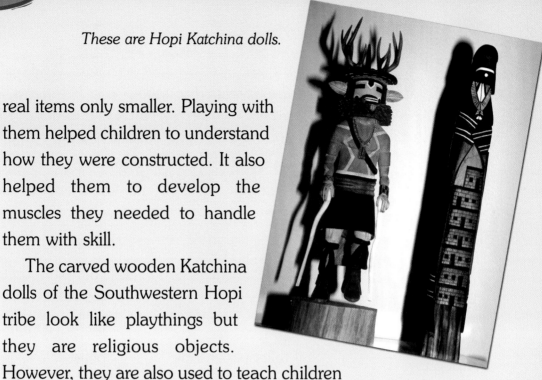
These are Hopi Katchina dolls.

real items only smaller. Playing with them helped children to understand how they were constructed. It also helped them to develop the muscles they needed to handle them with skill.

The carved wooden Katchina dolls of the Southwestern Hopi tribe look like playthings but they are religious objects. However, they are also used to teach children about their heritage. Stories passed down using string games or drawing games also taught children about traditional ways of life.

Still other toys were just for fun, such as noisemaking bull-roarers fashioned by the Indians from the Arctic or board games that involved elements of luck and chance.

The crafts in this book, from tribes around North America, let us use our imagination as we craft and play these games.

Pine Dancer Doll

Ojibwa are a large tribe spread throughout the Northeast. Their name means "puckered up." Trees served as landmarks for the Ojibwa. Young women of the tribe near woodland areas of the Great Lakes picked pine boughs from evergreen trees to craft fringy pine dolls. We will make this one out of feathers.

What You Will Need:

- scissors
- craft feathers
- pony bead
- ribbon
- pipe cleaner
- wood grain contact paper
- toilet paper tube
- colored pencils (optional)
- paper (optional)
- plate or cookie tray

1. Cut three or four craft feathers of the same length. Push the feather ends through a pony bead. Trim the bottom of the feathers so that they are even. Tie a ribbon around the middle.

2. If you wish, draw a small face and neck on a piece of paper with colored pencils. Cut it out.

3. Glue the face onto the top of the feathers, over the pony bead. Twist a piece of pipe cleaner to form arms.

4. Cover a toilet paper tube with wood grain contact paper. Glue the doll to the tube.

5. Stand your pine dancer doll on a plate or a cookie tray. Gently jiggle the plate or cookie tray back and forth. The dancer will appear to sway.

1. Put a pony bead on the end of three feathers. Tie a ribbon in the middle . . .

2. Draw a face . . .

3. Glue on the face and add a pipe cleaner for arms . . .

4. Cover toilet paper roll with contact paper and glue on the doll!

Yup'ik Story Knife Crayon Resist

Yup'ik live along the western Alaskan coast. Yup'ik means "real people." Though the area where they live is often cold and snowy, it does not freeze over during the long winter months. Children play outside, practicing yaaruin, or illustrated stories. It was a way of remembering and sharing tribal stories and values. Yup'ik girls illustrated the stories with symbols they carved into the mud or snow. The blunt knife they used to draw with was made of wood or ivory. The drawn symbols formed a picture language that would be crossed out or scraped away as the story progressed.

What You Will Need:

- construction paper
- dark crayons
- toothpick
- ribbon (optional)

1. Completely cover a light colored piece of construction paper with dark crayon. Press hard and add multiple layers of crayon until the surface is thick and shiny.

2. Use a toothpick to draw or scratch pictures in the crayon wax as you tell a story. Draw from left to right as you tell, crossing out symbols once you are finished with them.

1. Cover piece of colored paper with a dark crayon . . .

2. Use a toothpick to scratch pictures into the crayon wax . . .

3. Glue a ribbon on the top, and your story is ready for display!

Haida Painted Stick Game

Haida lived along the northwest coast of Alaska. They were known for their wood carvings. Haida craftspeople carved cedar trees into canoes, boxes, rattles, masks, and totem poles. They painted their carvings with minerals mixed into mashed salmon eggs. Black, red, white, light blue, and green were common paint colors. The oily egg paint both tinted and protected the wood. The Haida Painted Stick Game was played using forty to sixty finely carved and painted cedar sticks. These sticks were like playing cards. Play this streamlined craft stick version with a friend.

What You Will Need:

- 25 craft sticks
- placemat
- markers or poster paint

1. Use markers or poster paint to decorate twenty-four craft sticks. Make your own patterns. The last stick can be painted in stripes or left undecorated. This is the *djil*, or bait.

2. Let the sticks dry.

3. For game rules, see page 27.

This is a Haida bear mask.

1. Use markers or paint to decorate the craft sticks . . .

2. See page 27 for game instructions.

Kiowa Cradleboard Craft

Kiowa means "principal people." Kiowa were travelers. Originally from the northwest near the Columbia River, they migrated to Montana before settling Oklahoma and Texas. Cradleboards were backpacks used by American Indians for transporting babies. Different tribes made different cradleboards. Kiowa wrapped their babies in decorated hide bags. The bags were stuffed with dry grasses such as moss and cattail down. The bag was then mounted on boards that could be strapped to the back, leaned against a tree, or tied to a saddle.

What You Will Need:

- empty tissue box
- hole punch
- yarn
- fabric (optional)

- 2 paint stirrers or tongue depressors
- white glue
- beads (optional)

- colored toothpicks (optional)
- craft feathers (optional)
- straw (optional)

1. Place the tissue box vertically. Use a hole punch to punch four holes on each side of the oval opening.

2. Lace yarn through the holes, starting from the bottom. Turn the box over. Glue the two paint stirrers in a V-shape on the back. The ends of the "V" should jut out evenly at the top of the box. Let dry.

3. If you wish, decorate the area near the opening with beads or craft feathers. Or arrange varying lengths of colored toothpicks in patterns.

4. Line the inside of the box with soft fabric or straw. Place a doll or stuffed animal inside and lace to secure.

1. Start with a tissue box . . .

2. Punch holes around the opening and use yarn to lace it up . . .

3. Glue paint stirrers onto the back . . .

4. Decorate with beads and feathers!

Penobscot Birch Triangle Toy

Penobscot means "rock land." The Penobscot hunted and gathered for food. Tree bark was gathered regularly. They peeled the outer bark from the birch tree, which grew in the northeastern forests where they lived. By softening the bark in warm water, they could bend and sew it like cloth. Adults used the softened bark to make canoes, house coverings, food containers, and musical instruments. Children used it to make sleds and toys.

What You Will Need:

- scissors
- cardboard
- pencil
- puff paint (optional)
- white or wood-grained contact paper (optional)
- foil
- ruler
- string

1. Use scissors to cut a piece of cardboard into an eight-inch equilateral triangle. (See page 26 for the pattern.) Draw a three-inch circle in the middle of the triangle. Carefully cut out the circle.

2. Cover the cardboard with white or wood-grained contact paper, and paint designs if you wish.

3. Crumple a piece of foil into a ball that is no more than two inches in diameter. It must be able to pass through the hole in the cardboard triangle.

4. Cut a twelve-inch length of string. Tie one end of string around the middle of the foil ball.

5. Use the pointed end of the scissors to carefully poke a small hole near one corner of the triangle. Slip the other end of the string through the hole and tie it. See page 28 for game rules.

1. Start with a
foil ball . . .

2. Tie a piece of yarn
around the ball . . .

3. Cut out a
cardboard
triangle . . .

4. Decorate triangle and attach the other end
of the yarn. Your toy is ready for action!

Zuni Corncob Dart Game

Corn was an important crop for the Zuni, a tribe living along the Zuni River in New Mexico. Each year in December this southwestern tribe celebrated with a ceremony for the Corn Maiden spirits, who they believed introduced corn to their people. During this time, Zuni children may have played a throwing game using hoops made from corn husks. Darts thrown through the hoops were made with dried corncobs. Games played with hoops and spears, arrows, or darts were common to many American Indian tribes.

What You Will Need:

- yellow poster paint
- construction paper
- craft feathers
- plastic tray
- paper towel tubes
- hula-hoop
- ear of fresh or dried corn, husks removed
- white glue

1. To make the darts, pour yellow poster paint into a shallow plastic tray. Roll the ear of corn in the paint and use it as a stamp to make corn kernel patterns on the construction paper. Let dry.

2. Use scissors to cut the paper towel tubes in half.

3. Glue the painted construction paper onto the cut tubes.

4. Add craft feathers around one end of the tubes by gluing or taping them to the inside of the tube.

5. For game rules, see page 28.

This is a portion of a painting showing a ceremony for Corn Maiden spirits.

1. Pour some paint into a plastic tray . . .

2. Use a corncob to stamp a pattern on colored paper . . .

3. Glue stamped paper onto paper towel tubes and add some feathers . . .

4. Grab a hula-hoop and get ready to play!

Cree Cup and Pin Game

The Chippewa-Cree were fishers and hunters who lived in the sub-arctic before migrating to Montana. They lived in caribou- or moose-hide lodges, with a fire hole at the top that acted as a chimney. Cree children may have used shells or cone-shaped bones to make this version of a ring and pin game. Playing this game taught coordination skills helpful for spearing fish and animals.

What You Will Need:

- small paper cup
- crepe paper
- pipe cleaners
- beads

- crayons or markers (optional)
- scissors
- yarn

- unsharpened pencil
- clear tape

1. Glue crepe paper around the cup, and trim. If you wish, add pipe cleaners and beads.

2. Carefully poke a small hole in the bottom of the cup.

3. Thread a three-foot length of yarn through the hole so that the rim of the cup faces downward. Tie a knot at the top end of the yarn. This will ensure that the cup does not fall off.

4. Tie an unsharpened pencil at the bottom end of the string. Use tape to secure the pencil to the string.

5. To play, hold the pencil upright. Swing the cup up and away from you. Try to move the pencil so that the cup lands on it.

1. Decorate a cup with crepe paper, pipe cleaners, and beads . . .

2. Carefully poke a hole in the bottom of the cup . . .

3. Thread yarn through the hole and knot in place . . .

4. Tie a pencil to the other end of the yarn, and you are ready to play the cup and pin game!

Bannock Bone Buzzer

The Bannock and the Northern Shoshone lived on fish and wild plants they gathered in the grasslands of the Great Basin and along the Snake River in Idaho. They became skilled hunters and warriors after the Europeans introduced horses to them in the 1700s. Bannock children drilled holes in flat round animal bones or pottery pieces to make a buzzing spin toy. It works something like a two-handed yo-yo.

What You Will Need:

- two 1-1/4 to 1-1/2-inch metal washers
- poster paint
- scissors
- cardboard
- rubber cement
- string or yarn

1. Paint one side of each of the two metal washers using poster paint. Make them colorful. Let dry.

2. Cut a two-inch circle out of cardboard. (See page 26 for the pattern.)

3. With rubber cement, glue the nonpainted sides of the washers to the left and right sides of the cardboard circle.

4. Using the tip of the scissors, ask an adult to poke two holes through the center of the washers and through the cardboard. The holes should be 1/2 inch apart.

5. Cut a 20- to 24-inch length of string or yarn.

6. Thread one end of the string through one hole and the other end of the string through the second hole. Knot the ends.

7. For instructions on how to play, see page 29.

1. Use paint to decorate the washers . . .

2. Cut a circle out of cardboard . . .

3. Carefully poke holes through the centers of the washers and through the cardboard . . .

4. String everything together, and your disk is ready to spin away!

Cherokee Marble Game

Cherokee were farmers and hunters who lived in the southeast. They hunted with an atlatl, or short spear. Games they played often involved teamwork and throwing skills. Cherokee children made marbles from clay soil, round river rocks, or pine sap. They rolled them down logs to see which ones rolled farthest and fastest. Grownups chipped large stones to make marbles as big as billiard balls. They threw them at a set of holes in the ground. They tried to knock other team's marbles out of the way. Make your own marbles and then try the game.

What You Will Need:

- hardening clay
- white glue
- shoebox with lid
- poster paint
- scissors
- markers

1. Roll the clay into marble size balls. Make them as smooth and round as you can.

2. Let the marbles air dry. (Or follow the hardening directions for the clay.) Paint them in bright, swirling colors. Let dry.

3. Coat the marbles with a thin layer of white glue. This will seal the marbles and make them shiny. Let dry.

4. Use scissors to carefully cut a series of five holes slightly bigger than the marbles into the bottom half of the lid. The holes should form an L-shape. Use a marker to label the holes from one to five.

5. For instructions on how to play, see page 29.

1. Form your marbles out of clay. When dry, paint them bright colors . . .

2. Carefully cut out five holes in the lid of a shoebox . . .

3. Lean the lid against the shoebox, and you are ready to start playing!

Pomo Acorn Top

Pomo lived in coastal areas of California where large oak trees grew. Pomo children gathered acorns from oak trees each fall. Acorns formed a big part of their diet. They were shelled and boiled or mashed to make soup, bread, dyes, and medicines. Children spun them as tops. Use the acorn shape to make this top.

What You Will Need:

- hardening clay
- 3-inch stick or dowel
- toothpick
- poster paint (optional)
- white glue (optional)

1. Roll a chunk of clay into a two-inch ball.

2. Insert the stick into the center of the ball. One inch should stick out from the top.

3. If you wish, flatten a second chunk of clay into a flat circle. Use a toothpick to make an acornlike texture to the clay circle.

4. Mold the clay around the stick into a rounded triangular or acorn shape.

5. Place the circle atop the clay ball to look like an acorn cap. Let the clay dry. (Or follow the hardening directions for the clay.) If you wish, once the clay is dry or hard, paint it acorn-colors. Let dry. To make shiny, use a thin layer of white glue. Let dry.

6. Set the top on a flat surface. Roll the stick between your thumb and pointer finger. Let go.

1. Roll a ball of clay and insert a stick into the center . . .

2. Flatten another piece of clay to form the top of the acorn . . .

3. Place the flattened circle onto the clay ball . . .

4. When it dries paint it acorn colors. Your acorn top is finished!

Patterns

Use a copier to enlarge or shrink the design to the size you want.

Use tracing paper to copy the patterns on these pages. Ask an adult to help you cut and trace the shapes onto construction paper.

Bannock Bone Buzzer

At 100%

Enlarge by 200%

Penobscot Birch Triangle Toy

Game Rules

Haida Painted Stick Game

1. This is a two-person game. The object is to locate the *djil*, or bait, and collect the most sticks.

2. Player One divides all of the sticks into two handfuls. He or she shuffles each handful with his or her back turned away from Player Two.

3. Player Two chooses the hand he or she believes the bait is in.

4. Player One throws that handful onto the placemat. If the bait is there, Player Two keeps all of the sticks in the pile except for the bait. Player Two then divides the remaining sticks into two handfuls and shuffles them for Player One.

5. If the bait is not there, Player Two keeps nothing. He or she divides all of the sticks into two handfuls and shuffles them for Player One.

6. Repeat until the last pile is won. Then count the sticks. The player with the most wins.

27

Penobscot Birch Triangle Toy Game

1. To play, grasp a corner of the triangle opposite the string side.

2. Flip up the corner, tossing the ball into the air.

3. Try to move the triangle so that the ball drops through the hole.

Zuni Corncob Dart Game

1. This game is best played outside or in an big open room. Gather two or more players.

2. Have one person roll the hula-hoop along the ground or the floor.

3. As the hula-hoop rolls past, try to throw the darts through the hoop. Or try and knock the hula-hoop over with the darts.

Bannock Bone Buzzer

1. To play, hold one end of the string in each hand.

2. Hold the string parallel with the disk in the center. Twirl the string until it is tight. Or twirl the disk until the string is tight.

3. Then move both hands toward the disk and then quickly away as if you were playing an accordion. The disk will begin to spin.

4. Keep twirling the string and pulling away. This motion will keep the disk spinning. The weight of the washers aids the momentum of the disk.

Cherokee Marble Game

1. Turn the shoebox over. Prop the lid against the box so that it is at a slant.

2. Choose a number from one to five. Then roll a marble down the box lid, aiming for the hole with that number.

3. Keep score if you wish. Play alone or with friends.

Reading About

Books

Broida, Marian. *Projects About American Indians of the Southwest*. New York: Benchmark Books, 2004.

Clare, John D. *North American Indian Life*. Hauppauge, N.Y.: Barron's Educational Series, 2000.

Corwin, Judith Hoffman. *Native American Crafts of the Northwest Coast, the Arctic, and the Subarctic*. New York: Franklin Watts, 2002.

Dennis, Yvonne Wakim, and Arlene Hirschfelder. *Children of Native America Today*. Watertown, Mass.: Charlesbridge Pub., 2003.

Temko, Florence. *Traditional Crafts from North America*. Minneapolis, Minn.: Lerner Publications, 1997.

Trottier, Maxine. *Native Crafts: Inspired By North America's First Peoples*. Toronto, Canada: Kids Can Press, 2000.

Internet Addresses

Mythology of North American Indians

<http://www.windows.ucar.edu/tour/link=/ mythology/northamerican_culture.html&edu= elem>

National Museum of the American Indian

<http://www.nmai.si.edu/>

Index